TWENTY LESSONS
THAT
BUILD A
LEADER

TWENTY LESSONS
THAT
BUILD A LEADER

A CONVERSATIONAL MENTORING GUIDE

VINCE MILLER

EQUIP PRESS

Colorado Springs

First Edition: 2019
TWENTY LESSONS THAT BUILD A LEADER / Vince Miller
Paperback ISBN: 978-1-946453-63-1
eBook ISBN: 978-1-946453-64-8

EQUIP PRESS

Colorado Springs

TO: _____ Bob Ewing

FROM: _____ Janice Allen 5/6/19

NOTE:

_____ Let's build leaders!

TABLE OF CONTENTS

A NOTE FROM THE AUTHOR

Leadership is an experience that will test you to the core. Some days it will make you, and other days it will break you. This is because leadership is an experience that completely reshapes us. Some of the lessons you will discover in this book were passed on to me by numerous leaders over many years, but I had to learn the rest from my greatest mentor—failure.

My hope for you is that these lessons give you something to discuss with a friend, relative, coworker, or even your children. I hope they will stir a discussion that will give you an opportunity to proactively pass on wisdom. May this mentoring relationship lead to greater success as you lead your business, team, non-profit, church, or your very own family.

Join in a mentorship movement, and mentor or be mentored.

Keep moving forward,

USING TWENTY LESSONS THAT BUILD A LEADER

The Purpose

This 20-lesson guide is for mentors to use in private reflection or conversations with others. It's written to invite leadership and character development conversations for people of any age and can be used repeatedly.

The Process

First, build yourself

Read through one lesson each time and ponder privately on the reflection questions within the lesson. Each lesson uses the B.U.I.L.D. process.

- BEGIN with the goal.
- UNPACK your thoughts.
- INFORM through the Bible.
- LAND on action steps.
- DO one action for one week.

Second, partner up

Take each lesson further by partnering up with someone else. Use the 20 lessons as a mentoring tool that takes all the guesswork out of a leadership development conversation. Partner up with a friend, relative, co-worker, or someone in your family.

The Payoff

If you stay with the process for all 20 lessons, you will grow in character, in your leadership, and in community with others. Often we just need a plan to get moving. This book provides that plan—a method and a process that results in outcomes with a rich payoff.

SPEAKER & AUTHOR VINCE MILLER

Abandoned by his drug-using father at the age of two, Vince Miller grew up in a challenging and anxiety-producing environment. He endured the strain of his mother's two failed marriages as well as her poor choices and drug use. Fortunately, during Vince's formative teen years his grandfather, a man of faith, stepped up to mentor Vince, guiding him through a particularly difficult period.

Though he resisted initially, Vince became a follower of Christ at the age of 20. Soon after, he would be with his grandfather on his deathbed as cancer took his life. At that time, Vince committed before God to give back by mentoring men as his grandfather had mentored him. Vince's story demonstrates the importance of mentors to support others in overcoming the enormous hurdles that manhood, mentoring, fathering, and leadership present to a man who wants to live in faith and character.

Audiences respond to Vince's stories and teaching that motivate, convict, and sometimes even shock. He inspires men to lead and mentor others with an intelligent argument for faith and stories of choices he made as a man, husband, father, and leader.

After serving in notable organizations for over 26 years (including Young Life, InterVarsity, and TCU Football), Vince founded Resolute, a non-profit organization focused on providing men with tools for mentorship. He's written 16 books and Bible study handbooks, along with small group videos that are resources for mentorship. He also produces a daily writing known as The Men's Daily Devotional read by thousands daily.

If you are looking for a motivational and engaging communicator for your next retreat, conference, or event, reach out to Vince Miller directly through his website. www.vincemiller.com

Meaningful Integrity

"The supreme quality for leadership is unquestionably integrity.
Without it, no real success is possible, no matter whether it is on
a section gang, a football field, in an army, or in an office."

—DWIGHT D. EISENHOWER

"Whoever walks in integrity walks securely,
but he who makes his ways crooked will be found out."

—PROVERBS 10:9

Integrity is a challenge for everyone

Influential leaders are those who have successfully integrated their inner and outer lives so that they reflect one another. There's no contrast between who that leader is and how they behave. This integration is a lifelong pursuit that is gained slowly and lost rapidly—so it requires a persistent pursuit. When motivations match thoughts, thoughts match statements, and statements match actions, you have integrity (integration). Here are two levels of integrity and three marks of a person who has it.

Two Levels and Three Marks of Integrity

Level One | Congruent statements and actions

People can smell hypocrisy from a mile away. But leaders who do as they say with consistency make it easy for others to trust them and believe their message. If people can't count on your behavior to match up with your words, it's ultimately your words they'll find unreliable. As a result, you won't be able to convey to others what actions are acceptable and unacceptable.

Level Two | Motives are congruent with statements and actions

While many can see the external connection between what you say and what you do, there is another level of integrity. It's the integration between your motives and the things you say and do. Most will never know your motives unless you reveal them. Yet motivational integrity is integrity at the deepest level. This is a high calling and a great checkpoint for a leader. Great leaders conceal nothing and are readily willing to share their motives so that others can know the deepest level of their integrity. Purely motivated leaders make powerful leaders. Just consider this: Do you trust a leader whose motives are always in question?

Mark One | They welcome accountability

A leader that finds accountability laborious or resists legitimate feedback might have a gap in their integrity. On the other hand, a person who leads with integrity invites accountability and feedback. They have a disposition for accountability to ensure they don't lose ground with others, and even use accountability for their personal improvement.

Mark Two | They spend time with people of character

You are not only known by the people you keep company with, but they shape you. If you desire integrity in your work and personal life, then you must spend time with people of integrity so you can learn from them. Your company of friends and colleagues will either strengthen you or lead you to make compromises of character. Since character is more "caught than taught," you must always invest your time with people of the highest character; they will always make you better.

Mark Three | They practice integrity when no one's looking

What people see of your life is often like the tip of an iceberg. Much of life is hidden from the view of others, but the leader with integrity makes the same the decisions in private that they do in public. That is because deep-level integrity requires consistency everywhere—especially under the surface. These unseen decisions are the tell-tale sign of a truly integrated life.

Reflection & Mentorship

Begin

- When your motivations match your thoughts, your thoughts match your statements, and your statements match your actions, you have integrity.

Unpack

- What makes living a life of integrity challenging?
- You can almost immediately think of someone who has little integrity, but do you know someone who possesses a great deal of integrity? Describe why you identify them as such.
- How does the lack of integrity impact processes, products, and people? Try to be descriptive of the impact in each area.

Inform

- Speculate as to why Eisenhower called integrity the "supreme authority."
- The proverb above describes two ways in which you can walk. One may walk "securely" or one may walk a "crooked" path. How do these two terms describe the outcomes of a person who walks with and without integrity?
- Of the two levels of integrity above, which is more challenging—Level One or Level Two integrity?
- Of the three marks of integrity, which is hardest to live out in the workplace?

Land

- Let's face it: everyone lacks integrity. Which of the marks above is most elusive to you? Why?
- What steps do you need to take to live with greater integrity?

Do

- Commit to improving one mark of integrity listed above.

Discovering Values

"It's not hard to make decisions when you know what your values are."

—ROY DISNEY

"Blessed is the one who finds wisdom, and the one who gets understanding, for the gain from her is better than gain from silver and her profit better than gold."

—PROVERBS 3:13–14

Even though you don't state them, you have them

Everyone has values; the question is, do you know them? If not, you need to uncover them because this blind spot has the potential to undermine your leadership.

All of us live by values, whether they are spoken or unspoken. Values are the backbone of your external behaviors, attitudes, commitments, and decisions. And many times, these externals speak volumes about what you actually value. In the years I have known, consulted, and served under leaders, I've discovered that only a few can successfully describe and identify their values. This is a tragic truth for the state of modern leadership, mostly because stated values are the vital component of great leadership. Value alignment is a tell-tale sign of personal and leadership integrity. For example, when you align with an organization or people who do not support your personal values (known or unknown), you may be building a plan for career suicide. And on a personal level, when others hear you proclaim a particular value and then see you act out of line with it, they may perceive you as immature, incongruent, or manipulative. So the question is, how do you name and identify your personal values? The following are four questions that might help in determining yours.

Four Questions for Discovering Your Values

Mentors | Who has influenced your life?

There are leaders you admire and turn to for wisdom—they influence your life and leadership. You might call these people mentors. These mentors usually fit into one of three categories. First, passive mentors are the type that mentor us through their teaching and writing. For example, tens of thousands of people have heard Simon Sinek speak or read his books. He hasn't actually met most of these people, yet he is a passive mentor to them. Second, occasional mentors are the type that mentor you once in a while, often to help when you are facing a particularly difficult issue. These people might help strategize or troubleshoot a problem with us, but only on an irregular basis. Third, accelerated mentors regularly meet with us to coach us, hold us accountable, and encourage us to be better. They are deeply invested in us and are committed to your success. Each of us have people like this in our lives who have influenced us; their values have become our values, or they have helped us discover our own. Take some time to reflect on these three types of mentors and how they have shaped your life. See if you can list the truths they have passed onto you that are continuing to mold your life. These might be clues to your values. (Also, it might also be interesting to name a few leaders you don't admire or don't want to emulate as a way of discovering the values you don't hold.)

Life Crucibles | What has life taught you?

Everyone experiences a crisis at some point. This may be a financial crisis, a health crisis, a career crisis, or a crisis of faith. Each of these events has the power to shake you to the core and redefine what's valuable to you. For example, a financial crisis will reshape how you look at money and reveal its real value versus its assigned value. A career crisis will teach you that identity is not shaped by what you do, but by who you are. The school of hard knocks has the power to reshape your worldview and the things you value. So take some time to list a few life crucibles and consider what this pain has taught you. What personal values arose during this season? Pain, after all, is an influential teacher.

Pet Peeves | What irritates you?

Common everyday irritations are not to be confused with values. However, they often point to what you value. For example, if texting while driving irritates you, then maybe this indicates a value for human life. Or if sarcasm annoys you, perhaps you value dignity and encouragement. Anxiety-producing events help us to see our values in a raw and often emotional way. Consider listing a few pet peeves you have, identify why these irritate you, and name the value this indicates.

Deep Convictions | What has convicted you?

Every great leader has deep convictions that drive them. They wish to provide access to education or clean water, to protect life, to mend a social injustice, or to provide mentorship. That powerful conviction, whatever it may be, has the power to shape a positive future for yourself and others. It turns fear to faith, uncertainty to hope, and apathy to action for those around you. Martin Luther King Jr. believed in fighting for civil rights and equality as a Christian and activist because of his deep convictions, and his convictions carried him into leadership history. Consider your deep convictions and how they might be beneficial to the world.

What is needed in today's world are more leaders who live in line with their values. Be a leader of value by living out your values. Once you can name and identify your personal values, you can lead with confidence and conviction.

Reflection & Mentorship

Begin

- Values are the backbone of your external behaviors, attitudes, commitments, and decisions.

Unpack

- What does it mean when we say a service or product has value?
- What does it mean for a person to have value?
- What does it mean for a person to live from a set of personal values?

Inform

- Why would Disney say that decisions are "easier" when you know your values?
- The proverb above says that wisdom has value and that it is better than "silver or gold." Why would this be?
- Share one value you have learned from each of the four questions above.

Land

- Name three personal values you have.
- What steps do you need to take to live by these values?

Do

- Write down your values, define them, and live guided by them.

Building Credibility

"I don't have credibility, I'm a comedian."

—DENNIS MILLER

"Let your eyes look directly forward, and your gaze be straight before you. Ponder the path of your feet; then all your ways will be sure."

—PROVERBS 4:25–26

Stop undermining your credibility

Leadership is about you—or is it? In one sense, leadership is not about you because your success depends on the receptiveness of the people you are trying to serve, inspire, and equip. However, your success also depends to some extent on a skill that can be developed. But great leaders understand that titles, skills, tactics, and strategies of leadership only take them so far. The rest is dependent on the economy of their character, which has the potential to increase or decrease their credibility. I believe every leader eventually discovers that the most critical element of leadership is their own character—not just what they do, but who they are. Furthermore, they come to learn that even small cracks in their character have the potential to undermine all their credibility. This is true for both leaders and their organizations. Here are four key areas that contribute to building leadership credibility.

Four Areas that Build Credibility

Area One | Personal transparency

Transparency is a definitive currency of leaders because employees, volunteers, and customers instinctively want to know who the leader is. The greatest leaders I know have no difficulty being transparent with themselves and others. While some perceive transparency as a sign of weakness, great leaders understand that it takes tremendous confidence to open their soul up to others. On the other hand, non-transparent leaders eventually suffer an emotional disconnection from their followers, who view the leader as insecure or manipulative. By letting others into your life, you allow others to know you, which builds credibility and trust.

Area Two | Proven experience

Leadership credibility is built with proven leadership experience. There is no quick road to credibility, but it is made one leadership decision at a time—often over a long period of time. A variety of challenges must prove it. Sometimes this includes taking responsibility for mistakes, owning up to a blind spot, receiving critical feedback and growing from it, or giving away credit for success to someone else even when it leads to their advancement. In the process, you prove you are worthy to lead—sharing and enjoying success with others, learning from failure, and handling it gracefully. Proven leaders have trusted followers who are willing to believe in the decisions, fairness, wisdom, and ultimately the character of their leader. People do not expect their leaders to make the right calls all the time, but they do expect leaders to be honest about their mistakes, to take responsibility for what happened, and to learn from the experience a better way forward. It is in moments like these that leaders are proven—one decision at a time.

Area Three | Selfless vision

Leaders have a disposition toward a better future and cannot stop thinking about it. They have a vision for what can be, can often describe it in detail, and want to help others pursue it. They refuse to settle for what currently is, and call people to what potentially could be. They deflect attention from themselves to a higher cause, better future, and greater outcomes. But there's a caveat. Many visionary leaders can cast a vision yet cannot figure out how to get there. The greatest leaders I know not only have a vision, but they're willing to sacrifice to help others participate. They equip others regardless of the cost. Remember, a vision without a plan is merely a dream, and a vision without people is only a fantasy.

Area Four | Emotionally invested

Leaders inspire hope in others. They motivate, are profoundly optimistic about what can be, and call others to go with them. People who spend time with a true leader will come away inspired and encouraged, even in the face of uncertainty and challenge. This is because at the deepest level, a true leader is emotionally invested. This investment is more than a casual transaction; when leaders are fully invested, they motivate others to invest. This was the genius of leaders like Winston Churchill, a man who helped others believe what could be. In the darkest days of World War II, he motivated a whole nation to stand against Hitler and to never give up. Motivate and inspire someone today.

Reflection & Mentorship

Begin

- Credibility is the combination of what you do and who you are that is built over years and lost in seconds.

Unpack

- Why is credibility slow to build and fast to lose?
- Why do the titles, skills, tactics, and strategies of leadership only take a leader so far?

Inform

- Dennis Miller says he doesn't have credibility because of his occupation. Is this true or not?
- The proverb above says you are to "look" and "gaze" ahead. What do you think the author means by this?
- In which of the four areas do you excel, and in which do you need improvement? Be honest.

Land

- What credibility issues do you need to address?
- What steps do you need to take to increase your credibility?

Do

- Commit to one area above and boost your credibility.

Astute Discernment

"Discernment is not knowing the difference between right and wrong,
it is knowing the difference between right and almost right."

—CHARLES SPURGEON

"My son, do not lose sight of these—keep sound wisdom and discretion,
and they will be life for your soul and adornment for your neck. Then you
will walk on your way securely, and your foot will not stumble."

—PROVERBS 3:21 23

It's more than being smart, it's street smarts with character

Discernment is a vital and multidimensional leadership ability. Similar to wisdom, it's an ability that develops over time and is indispensable in the leadership of others. Discernment is a combination of cunning curiosity, uncompromising character, missional alignment, and the courage to act at the right time and in the right way. You acquire discernment through failure, which means you need to be keenly aware of your insecurities—it requires some grit to endure loss. You must possess the acumen to observe, synthesize, and translate information in a way that benefits those you lead and the mission you champion. And remember it's not about being smart—discernment is so much more.

Four Principles to Become a Discerning Leader

Principle One | Discerning leaders have a cunning curiosity

Great leaders ask the very best questions. Discernment requires an inquisitive nature and aspiration to advance in knowledge, understanding, and wisdom. Discerning leaders want to understand how their words will affect their stakeholders; they will take care not to lead others to flawed conclusions or into inappropriate action. Therefore they never make assumptions about their followers, but inquire about everything before concluding the best method of instruction. Discernment begins with gathering the best information.

Principle Two | Discerning leaders have uncompromising character

Leaders with discernment are people with an exceptional moral compass. They have integrated their thoughts, feelings, and actions with sound moral judgment. Leadership decisions made without regard to moral character will always injure people and damage organizations. Therefore, by remaining true to your convictions, you become a leader that others can trust in the workplace and beyond. And so, you have the potential to positively influence organizational cultures and an individual's personal choices.

Principle Three | Discerning leaders align character with mission

Discerning leaders don't just act—they act in alignment with both their personal character and organizational mission. They want to drive the purpose of the organization forward, but they want to do so in a way that brings out the best in them and in others. Therefore they never act independently of the mission they steward or independently from the character they profess. They choose to be conscious of shady transactions and decisions in business and life. In short, they use the full force of who they are to produce maximum impact. Anyone can be an employee, but discerning leaders align their character with the mission to influence and shape the whole enterprise.

Principle Four | Discerning leaders act with courage to win

Discerning leaders act to win. They have an inclination for action and an impulse for change. However, their actions reflect the ability to put disparate pieces of information together into a coherent whole and then make a decision. They are never indifferent or indecisive. Instead, their choices are carefully thought out and deliberately executed. And while they take risks, the risks are always calculated, having considered the potential unintended consequences. They act to win, and through this focus, they demonstrate visible forms of discernment.

Today as you lead, consider your discernment. Slow down and develop this ability. Give time to forge your character, competency, and skill in leadership from the inside out.

Reflection & Mentorship

Begin

- Discernment is a combination of curiosity, character, missional alignment, and courage to act at the right time and in the right way.

Unpack

- Is discernment something you are born with or something you develop? Defend your position.
- What characteristics does a person with discernment possess? Hint: Think of someone at work that possesses advanced levels of discernment.

Inform

- Charles Spurgeon, a well-known teacher, was surgical in his definition of discernment. In modern language, what did he mean by his statement above?

- The proverb above uses two vivid phrases to describe discernment: "life for your soul" and "adornment for your neck." What do these two phrases imply about the value of discernment?
- Of the four principles above, which needs improvement in your life? Share why, and be open and honest.

Land

- Sometimes in life, an event triggers an automatic response, and you fail to lean on discernment. Can you think of a recurring situation that provokes such a response in you?
- What steps do you need to take to increase your discernment?

Do

- Commit to one step of discernment.

Managing Conflict

"Peace is not absence of conflict,
it is the ability to handle conflict by peaceful means."

—RONALD REAGAN

"Hatred stirs up conflict, but love covers all offenses."

—PROVERBS 10:12

Conflict is inevitable—how you manage it matters

For anyone in leadership, conflict is inevitable. It will happen. And in some seasons it will feel like conflict management is the only thing you do. These conflicts may arrive in the form of a struggle over direction, a dispute between staff, or a disagreement with peers, customers, or suppliers. Since conflict is unavoidable, those who anticipate, lead, and successfully manage these moments have a distinct leadership advantage. The next time you encounter conflict, consider the five laws below.

Five Laws of Managing Conflict

Law One | Manage your anxiety

Conflict is not always bad, but you can become quickly bothered by it. This is part of the reason for increasing levels of leadership stress. You need to keep in mind that conflict is normal. Often it invites clarity where there is confusion and resolves a silent tension that needs to be made known. Many leaders are averse to conflict because they think conflict is a reflection on them and their leadership deficiencies. But what reflects poorly on a leader isn't conflict itself, but rather conflict poorly managed. If as a leader you can determine the root issues underlying the conflict without getting hooked by emotional insecurities, you will be able to lead more successfully through these encounters. Don't let yourself get baited and hooked. It's hard to help others resolve their anxiety when you feel it too.

Law Two | Listen and clarify

When emotions get elevated, people tend to stop listening to each other; their ability to listen is being hijacked by their emotional need to be heard. You can de-escalate a conflict by sitting down and listening—with precision—and clarifying what is being said. People want to be both heard and understood. In the process of listening, you are helping them to gain a voice and an audience they feel like they don't have, and at the same time you're developing a better understanding of what's happening in your organization. Make sure to give them time to ramp down emotionally before you conclude the listening session.

Law Three | Identify desired outcomes

As you listen, you should be on a quest to identify the outcomes you desire. Sometimes those in conflict with each other don't realize that they may have similar or even common goals, and are merely arguing over the best way to get there. If you know the result they both want, then you can help them figure out how they can get there—by working together. Remember, helping those you lead achieve the outcomes they want isn't as important as helping them learn lessons and deepen relationships through the conflict.

Law Four | State next steps (if necessary)

Is your next step another meeting with additional people? Is it a change in process or procedure? Is it seeking a new way of doing things? You need to identify the best course of action and ensure that those responsible are clear on what they need to do and when they need to do it. Set accountability in place to ensure that everyone follows through in doing their part to avoid another eruption. This should prove to all parties that you have responded appropriately to this situation, you are willing and able to reconcile future issues, and you are committed to helping others manage conflicts better themselves.

Law Five | Include outside counsel (when needed)

Sometimes you have parties who are unwilling to work toward a solution—or the solution involves parties outside of your authority or processes beyond your capacity to amend or modify. In such circumstances, you need to ask someone to help resolve the matter. Sometimes a human resource department needs to be consulted, or some other person or office with the power to make the necessary changes you cannot. Don't be afraid to ask others for assistance; it's better to show humility than to hide the issue or attempt to handle it on your own.

Remember that emotions and insecurities can prevent people from working through issues that are usually simple to solve. If you as a leader can help lower the emotional intensity of the parties and help them look objectively at the situation from the perspective of the desired outcome, solutions are often easy to find. Conflict is a healthy test, so embrace it as such.

Reflection & Mentorship

Begin

- Conflict is inevitable; therefore those who anticipate, lead, and personally manage these moments will have a distinct advantage.

Unpack

- What kinds of conflict do you prefer and not prefer?
- Is there a certain type of personality that gets you more anxious in times of conflict? Why is this so?

Inform

- Reagan's quote above is a great axiom. Why is this perspective hard to adopt when you're in conflict?
- The proverb above says love is powerful for conflict resolution. What does love have to do with conflict?
- Of the five laws above, which needs improvement in your organization, team, or personal leadership? Share why and be transparent.

Land

- What is one issue you need to address in how you handle conflict?
- What steps do you need to take?

Do

- Commit to incorporating one law of conflict this week.

Emotional Resilience

"The greatest glory in living lies not in never falling,
but in rising every time we fall."

—NELSON MANDELA

"A joyful heart is good medicine,
but a crushed spirit dries up the bones."

—PROVERBS 17:22

Learn to lead yourself by managing your emotions

One important characteristic of leadership is emotional resilience. It's the ability to be in touch with one's emotions and those of others. This includes the willingness to face your personal fears without being intimidated by outside pressure. Those with low emotional resilience allow their emotions to control, dictate, or govern their attitudes and actions. On the other hand, those with high emotional resilience are mindful of their feelings and those of others and as a result can effectively manage emotions rather than submitting to them.

Four Ways to Develop Emotional Resilience

One | Be emotionally aware

Critical to emotional resilience is the ability to be in touch with your emotions. If you experience feelings but are not in touch with them, they can undermine your leadership and elicit responses that adversely affect others. For instance, if you try to suppress or avoid the emotion of fear, its eventual emergence will elicit an immature response through which you might either hurt or hide from others. However, leaders who are emotionally aware of their fear and its triggers can learn to embrace and move through the experience in spite of their concerns for the benefit of the team. Awareness is where resilience begins.

Two | Face into fear

Emotionally resilient leaders have developed the ability to not only acknowledge their fear but to press through and operate in spite of what they feel. They are not crippled by fear of people, future, conflict, and uncertainty. It is important to develop this courage because there is always some level of fear when making key leadership decisions. What will people think? Will I face resistance? Will my team still trust me? What if our strategy fails? These and many other fear-based questions can paralyze a leader. Those with emotional resilience understand their fear but choose to move through it, taking measurable risks.

Three | Make right decisions

Resilient people not only are emotionally aware and move through their fears, but they also choose a course of action regardless of their concerns. This is because emotionally resilient leaders make the right choice even when it is not the convenient choice. Some leaders back away from making moral and ethical decisions, especially when it involves confronting a superior, compromising a personal agenda, or complicating a process. They may even fail to terminate an unproductive staff member, leave a partner with incompatible values, or release a high-paying customer that commands an excessive amount of time and energy. Acting out of fear is usually a deterrent to emotional resilience. But thinking right and taking righteous action will lead to right results.

Four | Play it forward

People with emotional resilience can do the right thing because they have developed the ability to think through the possible outcomes. In other words, they make calculated decisions after thinking through the unintended consequences. By doing their "homework ahead of time," resilient leaders minimize the negative impact of their choices, and therefore the risk, in decision making. This discipline takes into account the justifiable fears one might have, but reduces those fears by thinking through the possible consequences up front.

Reflection & Mentorship

Begin

- Emotionally resilient leaders are mindful of their feelings but effectively and appropriately manage them rather than allowing them to control their actions and reactions.

Unpack

- Do leaders have to have emotional resilience to be a great leader? Why or why not?
- Do you know a leader who appears to have a lot of emotional resilience? What do you like about them as a leader?

Inform

- Nelson Mandela "fell down" and suffered through many difficulties, including decades of imprisonment, before rising to lead the people of his country. Do you feel like the world lacks leaders like him who are resilient over a lifetime?

- In the proverbial statement above, it states a "joyful heart is good medicine." How is joy that dwells in a person's heart an anecdote for emotional issues and problems? Is this simply the power of positive thinking or is it something more?
- Which of the four aspects of emotional resilience do you need to give attention to become a more effective leader?

Land

- What issues have come to mind for you today?
- What steps do you need to take to address these issues?

Do

- Take on one resilience building activity this week.

Effective Storytelling

"The thing that I took away as an early fan from Bob Dylan was the storytelling aspects. He can tell some wicked stories."

—ED SHEERAN

"And [Jesus] said, 'There was a man who had two sons.'"

—LUKE 15:11

Make a memory with a story

Storytelling is a communication tool that's more powerful than most leaders recognize. People are 22 times more likely to remember a story than communication that relies heavily on data, facts, quotes, statistics, or figures. This is why great leaders lean on great stories. Take Jesus for instance. Who can forget the stories he told over 2,000 years ago about a Good Samaritan and a Prodigal Son? Even people who have never read the Bible know the general thesis, points, and outcomes to these timeless stories. Many people even reference these parables in everyday life, without ever having read them. Whether you believe in Him or not Jesus is still one of the world's great leaders and told stories frequently as a leader. His famed stories, and his leadership example, have stood the test of time.

For leaders, storytelling is crucial at every level of an organization. People emotionally connect with stories, and therefore remember its importance, value, and outcome longer than they will an internal memo, white paper, lecture, or company talk down. Regardless of who you lead, whether stockholders, customers, cross-functional teams, or volunteers, a well-told story will do far more to inspire and motivate than you realize. The following are four tips for conveying a compelling story.

Four Tips of Effective Storytelling

One | Make it real, transparent, and authentic

Embellished stories will be quickly perceived as inauthentic. Instead, tell real stories with real people and real outcomes. For example, a story of an employee going the extra mile to win over a customer will communicate far more than demanding that employees go the extra mile. An authentic note from a real customer, positive or negative, will be remembered far more than a list of bullet points on proper customer service. And a transparent story of your real leadership failures, shortcomings, weaknesses, and challenges will do more to unite you with subordinates and superiors than you realize.

Two | Build a problem

Leaders love problems because they're only opportunities that need better solutions. So tell a story about the problem and describe it in detail. Maybe it was a customer in desperate, immediate need for a product. Or a team working against impossible odds. Or both. Remember these problems demand solutions, and the heroes in the stories are those characters who figure out a way to deliver a heroic solution. Building a story around these problems requires heroes and heroic moments to resolve the tension. And these stories motivate others to become a solution provider or hero in their area of influence.

Three | Sell the solution, not the transaction

Transactions are essential to companies and its employees, yet are often uninspiring. But solutions provided to customers in the transaction can inspire companies, employees, customers, and people in the outside world. In storytelling, don't focus on the transaction itself, but the solution provided in the transaction. A description of a transaction tends to involve facts, figures, statistics, and processes, which focus on metrics. However, solutions that include these metrics drive storytelling beyond the transaction itself and toward something emotional. Solutions are the reasons customers are loyal to your business, so don't get lost in the transaction. Prosperous companies are focused on the solutions—so sell it in your story.

Four | Refine and retell the story

Once you have a few great stories, refine them and tell them again and again. You may worry that people have already heard all of your stories, but ignore this self-talk and tell them again. Perpetually tell them until the story hardens into the hearts of your people and into the foundation of your organization's culture. Stories define a culture, so your best stories are a quick way of reminding people of the culture you are developing. For example, consider the values of your company. Can most of your people remember them? Probably not. But what if you used a few great stories to attach word pictures to these values? Stories make them much more likely to recognize and therefore easier to live out. Attach your values, strategies, goals, and vision to stories and tell them continually.

Given the power of story, leaders ought to put as much time into how they communicate stories as they do anything else. If you want your message remembered, don't merely give a report—tell them a story.

Reflection & Mentorship

Begin

- Great leaders tell great stories to connect, inspire, and motivate others.

Unpack

- How often do you hear leaders tell stories? Can you recount a few memorable ones?
- What is a positive or negative story you often tell in your leadership of others? What point does it make as you inspire and motivate others?

Inform

- Bob Dylan was a great storyteller. Can you remember one of the stories of his songs?
- Can you remember the story, characters, tension, and solution in the story of the Prodigal Son?
- Where do you need to grow in your storytelling as a leader?

Land

- What concerns do you have about leading through storytelling?
- What steps do you need to take to overcome these concerns?

Do

- Tell a story, or a few, this week as you lead and take note of people's responses.

Leadership Health

"If you want to go quickly, go alone.
If you want to go far, go together."

—AFRICAN PROVERB

"Be not wise in your own eyes."

—PROVERBS 3:7

Leaders examine their personal health

It's possible to get a read on the health of almost any leader. Usually, this is determined by a variety of factors including their honesty, integrity, openness, and willingness to have candid conversations. Staff members always have a read on their leaders. They know when a particular subject matter is taboo to discuss in the presence of their manager or leader. This taboo subject matter is a definitive indicator of insecurities and can result in a leader demonstrating narcissistic tendencies such as authoritative control and excessive micromanagement. However, the greater your willingness to address issues in the culture and your leadership, the healthier you will be. Remember that the best leaders will allow and even encourage their staff to put issues on the table even if it is about them. The following are two factors indicative of leadership health.

Two Factors of Leadership Health

One | Unthreatened self-worth

Leaders with high levels of health are leaders who foster a "nothing to prove, nothing to lose, and nothing to hide" attitude. In other words, they are not afraid of pushback, criticism, suggestions, or change. When in the wrong, they do not get defensive, over-explain, and blame others. Sometimes they will own up and even take the heat for someone else's mistake on the team. And because they have nothing to prove, it's okay if team members get something wrong. But it is also okay if a subordinate gets the credit too. Their pride or ego is equally unaffected by wins or losses. They are far more concerned about how they consistently play the game. Anyone with this attitude is a leader who cares deeply about their leadership and the impact it has on people and therefore is unthreatened personally.

Two | Openness to dialogue

What does it mean to invite open dialogue? It means that other than personal attacks or issues that hijack the given agenda, any problem is free for discussion. And why? Because leadership is not about a win for a single person but for the mission of the organization. Therefore, issues openly discussed result in solutions that must be addressed. Open dialogue about issues allows a team and leader moments to bond. The best leaders foster this kind of public discussion around their table. There are no issues that cannot be raised with the two exceptions above. It is evident that this type of leadership requires a leader with a non-defensive posture. But if you live by the value that you have nothing to prove, nothing to lose, and nothing to hide, robust dialogue becomes possible—you can even handle comments about yourself or a leadership adjustment that you need to make.

The key to both of these values is that the leader must live them out. When the staff finally comprehends that their leader lives non-defensively and is not threatened by those who disagree with them or even criticize them, they will start to do the same. It's in this kind of culture that the best decisions are made because it invites high levels of candid conversation and honesty. If you lead, consider making these two values present in your leadership circle. But be prepared to swallow your pride and become less defensive.

Reflection & Mentorship

Begin

- The greater your willingness to address issues in the culture and your leadership, the healthier a leader you will be.

Unpack

- What adjectives would you use to describe the healthier leaders you know?
- What adjectives would you use to describe the unhealthy leaders you know?
- What are the notable differences between the two?

Inform

- The African proverb suggests "distance" is a notable difference between the two styles or approaches of leadership. Why?
- The second proverb states, "Be not wise in your own eyes." Why would this be a factor in the long-term health of a leader?
- Of the two factors above, which is vital for you at this point in your leadership: unthreatened self-worth or openness to dialogue?

Land

- What issues do you need to address to increase your leadership health?
- What steps need to be taken immediately?

Do

- Find a leader who has traversed the issues you've identified and talk with them about how they have achieved success.

Enlisting Others

"Leadership is the art of getting someone else to do something you want done because he wants to do it."

—DWIGHT EISENHOWER

"Wealth gained hastily will dwindle,
but whoever gathers little by little will increase it."

—PROVERBS 13:11

Are people actually following you because they want to?

Extraordinary leadership is not about you. In fact, it's not about your skill, talent, or ability. It's not even about your self-proclaimed superior vision that is going to take the world by storm. Extraordinary leadership occurs when followers enlist to a vision you have cast and vote to embrace it on their own. As the leader, you help people see, experience, and realize a better future that they want to accomplish. Leaders know how to enlist others in a vision greater than themselves that may never be entirely achieved. Here are some fundamental principles leaders understand about enlisting others.

Four Principles of Enlisting Others

Principle One | Followers select leaders

Those who follow a leader always voluntarily choose to follow. Leaders don't select followers, even though from your perspective this may appear to be the case. When a person decides to follow a leader, they are usually motivated by these two factors. First, the leader articulated a vision that the follower embraced, which is a big deal because some leaders lack proper vision. Second, the follower decided that the leader is someone who is worth following. This is where the consistent character of the leader is essential. And when a leader casts compelling vision and demonstrates consistent character, others enlist in the two most valuable commodities in leadership—what they say and who they are.

Principle Two | Leaders persuade

Great leaders don't resort exclusively to command and demand; they persuade and influence. There's a tremendous difference. Command demands that you fall in line, but influence persuades you to follow of your own will. While there are times command and demand must be practiced, especially in life-or-death situations, a leader must also understand when to use persuasion to influence behavior. Leaders persuade people to work together, to achieve more, to reach for improbable goals, and to put personal interests aside. They essentially convince people to change their mind. And since changing people's minds is both an emotional and intellectual venture, persuasion is the predominate tool required to enlist others.

Principle Three | Leaders invest in people

Remember, leadership is not about you, but instead is a cause others are enlisted in. Yet, it is about you in that it's your responsibility to invest in people, so that they can successfully realize the vision they joined. You are a steward, not an owner of the vision, the process, and the people who live out that vision. As a steward, it's your primary responsibility to pour yourself into people so that they can realize the full potential of the vision they embrace and move the mission forward. But that only happens with a large amount of investment in others.

Principle Four | Leaders develop new competencies

Competency in leadership is essential to enlisting others. Leaders advance in leadership by developing new competencies along the leadership path. While leadership is not all about skills, tactics, strategies, or a slew of other competencies, people will not enlist to follow incompetent people. There are amazing leaders in our world today, some who hit a leadership ceiling because they fail to develop new competencies. But exceptional leaders understand that there is always something new for them to learn. They have a keen and humble awareness that they don't know it all. They understand that their leadership needs constant honing and development. Remember, people choose to follow a leader. And they can also choose not to follow.

Reflection & Mentorship

Begin

- Leaders know how to enlist others in a vision greater than themselves that may never be entirely achieved.

Unpack

- Do you agree that followers select leaders rather than the other way around? Why or why not?
- How capable is your team (scale 1–10) at enlisting others in the group's mission and vision?

Inform

- Dwight Eisenhower understood something that most leaders fail to understand. Why do we forget this important principle about leadership?
- What is meant by the adage above that states, "whoever gathers little by little will increase it?" How is this methodology for investing similar to the process of enlisting others?
- Of the four principles above, which do you excel at and which do you need to develop?

Land

- What issues do you need to address as a leader to further enlist others?
- What steps need to be taken?

Do

- List the people who follow you and what they need from you to be fully enlisted.

Building Accountability

"The best kind of accountability on a team is peer-to-peer. Peer pressure is more efficient and effective than going to the leader, anonymously complaining, and having them stop what they are doing to intervene."

—PATRICK LENCIONI

"Iron sharpens iron, and one man sharpens another."

—PROVERBS 27:17

Don't fight it; you were designed for it

In spite of the images of the rogue individualist that you see frequently modeled in media by leaders, you were designed for relationships. Even the strongest and most rugged leader needs others to live life well and to gain traction in any part of their life. While everyone prefers to do life alone because of the assumed benefits, you are not better alone—you are always better together. In fact, adversaries and allies both have the potential to draw out positive attributes through accountability that make you a better leader. The question you have to ask yourself is are you willing to subject yourself to the type of accountability that has the potential to make you better? Here are some ways that you can build accountability into your life.

Five Steps to Building Accountability

One | Quit avoiding relationships and instead seek them out

Leaders can be intensely private about their inner lives. Sometimes this protective posture is just plain old pride. This pride keeps leaders from getting in touch with their deeper needs or taking the step of sharing these needs because they expose potential weaknesses. When it comes to accountability, it is often pride that prevents advancement—hubris in its most elusive and insidious state. Humility says, "I need to be in a relationship," while pride says, "I don't want to expose myself." This issue is directly related to the next truth.

Two | You need to invite honest feedback

As humble leaders, you should be willing to invite feedback so that you can get help where you struggle. The first step is admitting this need to yourself—rather than pretending you possess all the wisdom you need. And the second step is inviting others to help in the situations where you don't know how to help yourself. But remember, you only invite this feedback when you have authentic and trusting relationships established.

Three | Ask for specific accountability

There is no human being who doesn't need accountability. All of us have different struggles and unique vulnerabilities, and without authentic relationships with others, you will never become better. But here is the thing about accountability—you have to be specific to see specific results. You have two paths to choose from on this step. You can avoid specific accountability—call it "accountability"—and walk a broad path with loose descriptions and obscure goals. Or you can start asking for specific accountability and walk a narrow path with tight descriptions and actionable goals. And it's the narrow path that produces better returns. When you invite another person to hold you accountable in areas of weakness, even when it's embarrassing or painful, you get better at facing the challenge of accountability, and you will get better results from accountability. So make accountability specific and measurable so you know what it looks like when you win and when you lose.

Four | Make accountability positive rather than negative

Many resist accountability because it suggests you have to submit to dictatorial people and submissive relationships that often point out all our deficiencies. But accountability is not only about commanding submission, enduring discipline, or exposing inadequacy. There is another way of looking at accountability that is far more positive. It is one that invites challenge with positive returns. It's one that asks, "Can we hold each other accountable and mutually encourage each other as we get better together?" Keep in mind accountability might be better understood as "encouraging one another." Turn accountability away from these negative paradigms and toward more positive ones.

Five | Celebrate small marks of success

You will never "arrive" in your leadership, as it's a never-ending pursuit. However, every small step you take to grow is one step toward a better tomorrow. Define and mark small steps, and keep taking them as all of those incremental steps lead to significant growth. Celebrate them one at a time.

Reflection & Mentorship

Begin

- You are designed for relationship and accountability, and the positive friction between these has the potential to make us better as leaders.

Unpack

- Do you agree that accountability mostly has a negative understanding, tone, and application?
- What can you do to welcome more positive and optimistic forms of accountability?

Inform

- Patrick Lencioni makes an interesting comment above about "peer-to-peer mentoring." Why is this a better option in his opinion?
- The proverb above says that iron sharpens iron. What happens when iron grinds against other metal? What happens when the iron is exposed to the elements and is not active or used?
- Which of the five steps of accountability triggered learning for you?

Land

- What issues do you need to address to welcome accountability?
- What steps do you need to take to build accountability?

Do

- Invite someone to hold you accountable for one measurable action and report your results.

Decision Making

"Be willing to make decisions. That's the most important quality in a good leader. Don't fall victim to what I call the 'ready-aim-aim-aim-aim syndrome.' You must be willing to fire."

—T. BOONE PICKENS

"Without counsel plans fail,
but with many advisers they succeed."

—PROVERBS 15:22

Come on, it's time to make a decision

Leaders are required to make decisions; as the leader and organization grow and the complexity of the decisions increase, the results take on more impactful consequences. Three potential pitfalls are not making necessary decisions, making decisions without the required counsel, or putting off the decision until every detail is perfect. Great leaders will tell you that they have made far more bad choices than perfect ones, but they will also tell you that they learned from every bad decision, allowing them to make more good choices as time progressed. As a leader, you should be conscious of the four standard methods of decision making and the pros and cons of each.

Four Methods of Decision Making

One | Command

Here, decisions are made unilaterally by the leader without the involvement of others. In certain command structures, like the military, people with the power to make decisions must act promptly within their area of influence to resolve an issue. The upside is decisions get made quickly. However, sometimes command decisions carry a downside. Without the voice and counsel of others, you may be surprised by the unintended consequences of the judgment. The people you lead may come to feel a lack of ownership. Command decision making is efficient and effective but can feel unilateral, circumventing the opportunity for teamwork. But used in the right circumstances, it gets things done.

Two | Consult

In this case, a leader makes the final decision but consults with others in the decision-making process. Generally, consulting with the right team members or stakeholders is a smart decision. Others will suggest options, share ideas, see issues, or have opinions you may not have thought of, and may well suggest modifications or alternative paths that complement the views you hold. There is rarely a downside to consulting with the right people in the decision-making process, provided it is appropriate for them to hear the information you are sharing. The key is to consult with the right people who will give sound counsel.

Three | Vote

Voting is a conventional method of executing decisions on boards made up of partners or directors that are working together toward a joint mission. Usually, voting is used in situations where a group process is mandated or where more than one person is ultimately responsible for the decision made. Church boards or a group of partners often make decisions by vote. But this can also be true of a workgroup that is responsible for a project. Used in the right situations and the right way, voting is an excellent way to decide on a path so that the group can move forward.

Four | Consensus

In consensus, a group will discuss and debate until there is general agreement to move in a confident direction together. Consensus sometimes means a group will unanimously agree. But not always. Sometimes they will only generally or reluctantly agree, lacking better options. Here you need a deliberate process to arrive at a consensus; in the end, stakeholders are usually the ones making the final decision and announcement to teams, employees, or the organization as a whole. This type of decision making ensures that boards or groups are operating in harmony, and it is the decision-making process often used on senior teams. This process works best where you have other individuals who know how to work together well.

In this end, great leaders will use different decision-making processes in different situations. Knowing which to use in specific circumstances is how leaders make the very best decisions.

Reflection & Mentorship

Begin

- Leaders are required to make decisions; as the leader and organization grow and the complexity of the decisions increase, the results take on more impactful consequences.

Unpack

- What is the positive impact of decision-making on your team?
- What are the negative ramifications of bad decisions on your team?

Inform

- What is the point T. Boone Pickens makes above?
- The proverb suggests that "counsel" is important. In what ways do you involve counsel in your leadership today that you have not in the past?
- Which of the four types of decision-making processes above do you use the most? Which one do you need to use more?

Land

- What decisions do you need to make today?
- Which method above do you need to deploy?

Do

- Deploy a method above, make a decision, and see it through.

Engaging Media

"Whoever controls the media, controls the mind."

—JIM MORRISON

"There is one whose rash words are like sword thrusts,
but the tongue of the wise brings healing."

—PROVERBS 12:18

Don't ignore it–– it's powerful, so figure out how to use it

Leadership carries power and position, and because of this, you are given a platform to inspire others to action. A leader of character knows that this comes with a heavy responsibility to effectively engage media—a skill that must be cultivated. Media venues at your fingertips today (blogs, videos, social platforms, and podcasts) are used to communicate a message that will be heard by many audiences. If you ignore the influence of media, the tool of media, or your emotional response to media, then you'll end up leaving a lot of your leadership potential on the table. At the other end of the spectrum, the overuse and improper use of media can generate annoyances with your audience. So you must find ways to successfully leverage this tool.

Five Ways to Engage Media

One | Produce compelling content

Too often in using the media, you think about producing content when you need to be thinking about producing compelling content. There is always a difference between what you believe is valuable to communicate and what your audience thinks is valuable. If you don't deliver what's compelling to your audience, the messages will be ignored. Understanding what motivates and compels your audience is vital to compelling messaging content. Here's a quick tip: grab your audience emotionally by reaching out to their hopes and dreams, not yours. Put them at the center of the story and they will be more engaged.

Two | Properly disseminate

It's good to consider how you will spread your message. The key is to adopt a method that will work for the target audience and for the type of content you have to deliver. Is it a memo or a meeting? Is it a webinar or a training event? Should you say it over social media or should your remarks be delivered in person? Do you give the content away for free or do you charge? Is it satire or serious? Do you need to be professional or funny? Consider your options and disseminate appropriately.

Three | Pace appropriately

Sometimes business goals will have us working at a pace that outperforms our messaging. But the message doesn't have to keep up the pace. The world today is inundated by content and messages; people can only tolerate so much. You have to moderate the pace. If all you ever broadcast about is one topic, then people will stop listening. On the other hand, if you don't talk about it enough, then people won't remember. You have to find a good pace for your message, one that is paced at the speed of consumption. Consider a pace that is consumable by your audience, and be systematic about revealing the message one phase at a time.

Four | Social media engagement

Social media creates and invites the opportunity for interaction. It is not just for posting ideas, pictures, and thoughts you have, but for encouraging discussion and engagement with others. Most ignore the power of the social media conversation, therefore posting in a way that shuts down a dialogue rather than inviting discussion. The best use of social media invites dialogue that lets others become the center of the conversation. Also, as you use social media for personal engagement, you need to realize not everything needs to be posted. While you might think your feed only represents you, it might adversely affect your business, character, relationships, and reputation to the world.

Five | Enable freedom

As a leader, you need to help people understand how to use media. Today you need to give people a reliable understanding of what is appropriate and inappropriate. Media can be powerful in both a positive and negative way—so don't just tell people what you don't want them to do. Show them what to do. In media today, with new forms and growing platforms, teach people how to do engage with and leverage technology to make life easier. If you show them how, they will learn healthy patterns of engagement.

Reflection & Mentorship

Begin

- Leaders use media effectively to engage followers, but it's a skill that must be cultivated.

Unpack

- How have you seen leaders ineffectively use media?
- How have you seen leaders embarrass themselves on media?
- What is the impact of both above?

Inform

- Do you agree with Jim Morrison's statement on the power of media?
- The proverb suggests that there is something different between "rash words" and a "wise tongue." What is it?
- Which of the five points above do you feel leaders violate the most? Why is this so?

Land

- How do you need to leverage the media differently?
- What steps do you need to take today?

Do

- Use a form of media as a tool for leadership this week.

Receiving Feedback

"Feedback is the breakfast of champions."

—KEN BLANCHARD

"Whoever loves discipline loves knowledge,
but he who hates reproof is stupid."

—PROVERBS 12:1

You have blind spots, but do you see them?

Everyone has blind spots. This is something you discover this in driver's education class; you have gaps in your vision as you drive down the road. You have a forward view, side-view mirrors, and rear-view mirrors that each give us perspective on the surroundings. But even with the help of side and rear-view mirrors, ten to fifteen percent of your environment remains outside of your view. These are your blind spots.

You also have blind spots in your life, both in our leadership and character. What's interesting is that other people see your blind spots just fine, but you tend to see this as a threat instead of an opportunity. Instead of looking to others for illumination into this part of yourself, you may choose to stay in the dark out of fear. Fear of others, fear of truth, fear of change, fear of transparency, and fear of admitting weakness or fault. But what you often fail to realize is that when others point out your blind spots, their motivation is usually for your betterment. You need this feedback to discover what is holding you back as a leader. But accepting this sort of assistance doesn't use a natural leadership muscle. It's one that must be developed.

Four Principles on How to Receive Feedback

One | Listen to your emotions

When we're receiving feedback, it's almost an automatic response to emotionally ramp up. Often you will respond by blaming others or trying to explain ourselves. But you need to bite your lip in these moments. When your pulse begins to race and your body starts to signal biological responses like sweating, blushing, or muscle tension, you need to take a moment and quiet your emotions. Reduce the impulse in these moments to self-preserve and try not to see the person delivering the feedback as an adversary.

Two | Listen thoroughly

Rather than respond too quickly, listen completely to someone giving you feedback. People are not always so good at delivering constructive criticism— just as you may not be great at receiving it. So give the giver an opportunity to explain what they see. It's also good to invite them to clarify or restate their perspective, or to give examples as you listen. Just let them talk and get everything out. You may find they have been thinking about this for a while. If you demonstrate receptivity, they are likely to soften their tone and bring a more positive perspective to the feedback they're giving. And don't prepare an answer in your mind; instead pay attention entirely to them. Ask them to give illustrative examples. Remember they are not the enemy. The problems they see are just opportunities to find better solutions.

Three | Ask for suggestions for improvement

To help a person move from raw feedback to constructive feedback, ask them to give examples of how they might handle the issue or what they might do to improve. Since they see the problem differently than you, it might benefit you to hear their perspective. When you explicitly ask them to proceed, you're winning them over to a positive view and inviting them to help you to become better.

Four | Thank and apologize

There is usually an opportunity to apologize. When appropriate, you should do so—without blaming or explaining. Own up to your issues; everyone has them because no one is perfect. And then tie a nice bow on the end by thanking them. A genuine word of gratitude will give them the courage to come to you again with their insights. It will signal that you want a healthy, open, transparent, and authentic relationship with them as well. And they might have something amazing to report back to other peers about your courage and willingness. But thanking them helps to bring closure for you so that you can move forward. While you are sure to think on what was said for a while, the moment will be over for your acquaintance—their words are now yours to learn from and move through.

As a leader, you must find the courage to both give and receive feedback. How you receive that feedback matters. So develop the skill and ability to invite feedback from others, because this is what accelerated leaders do. Build a culture of positive feelings toward feedback, and you will become a better leader and develop a healthier culture.

Reflection & Mentorship

Begin

- Personal growth happens when you locate blind spots with the help of a little feedback. But it's not a natural leadership muscle to ask for help of this kind. It's one that must be developed.

Unpack

- What do people do who are not receptive to feedback?
- How developed is your business culture at both giving and receiving feedback?
- What could be done to invite a culture of feedback?

Inform

- Blanchard's quote is critical; what's another way to say what he said?
- The proverb suggests that the person who hates reproof is stupid. Why would this be so?
- Which of the four principles is most challenging for you?

Land

- What personal issue do you need to address immediately to get better at receiving feedback?
- What steps do you need to take today?

Do

- Invite someone to give you feedback, and subject yourself to the process above.

Exceptional Writing

Leaders are writers, so why aren't you writing

In today's fast-paced world, how you present yourself and your ideas in writing can have a powerful impression—whether it be positive or negative. The ability of a leader to communicate well in writing is critical for superiors, boards, employees, and customers. Many leaders are ineffective at this necessary and essential skill. Nothing will dismiss your voice like a poorly-written email, a counterproductive letter, a defectively-drafted post, or even an unprepared speech containing language or wording that hijacked the main point. Writing remains vital, and this will not change. As you improve in articulating your ideas, people will have a better understanding of where you are trying to lead them to, and the whole enterprise will be far more effective.

How Writing Benefits the Leader

One | Writing synthesizes random thinking

While there are many forms of communication today in our digital world, the written word still matters. Presidents and officials in countries around the globe communicate from written notes and teleprompters because every word matters. And it is in writing that you arrange your thoughts, words, ideas, and images into thoughtful patterns that people can hear, understand, and act upon. While casual, impromptu communication has its place, a well-prepared communication will always be the most effective method of transferring information to other people. Whenever you can take time to slow down and carefully build a message word by word, your team will benefit from the investment.

Two | Writing simplifies the complex

Writing also helps to clarify often complex reasoning. It does take time and effort to do this, but when you write your thoughts out you have to think about how people will read, hear, and interpret each word. As you write, your mind often slows to clarify complications, reducing them to essentials insights that are easy for people to understand. The organization of thoughts and concepts is an inherent part of writing. Writing declutters so you can clarify for others.

Three | Writing values attention and does not waste it

With all the competing information that our teams, boards, and staff come across daily, it is easy to become confused and distracted—wasting valuable time and attention. A person's attention span is not infinite. Each person you speak to has a limited amount of time available to them that day, and their attention is valuable. Be concise; don't waste their time with useless conversation, pointless email, or a time-sucking report. In today's world, content is no longer king; now precise and excellent content is king. When a leader comes along who can cut through the static, clearly state a plan or concept, and simplify complex ideas, people listen and respond.

Four | Writing should be kept plain, not made complicated

Writing should always be plain: clear in its content, easy to read, devoid of complicated words, and written so a modern reader can understand and know exactly what to do. To ensure that your writing is understandable, it is a good idea to have one or two people from a variety of perspectives preview communications and offer suggestions. Sentence fragments, vague words, subject and verb disagreement, misspellings, comma misuse, and complicated words can and will be a distraction. So keep it plain.

You will need to practice—and practice a lot. But the more you write, the better you get.

Reflection & Mentorship

Begin

- The better you can articulate your ideas as a leader, the better people will hear and the more effective you will be as you lead.

Unpack

- Do you think writing is as vital a skill for leaders as it has been in the past?
- List a few writings that have shaped the world as you know it today.
- What is the impact of great writing?

Inform

- Stephen King, who helped to shape modern culture, finds reading and writing equally vital; why do you think the link between reading and writing is important? Or is it less relevant today?

- Take a guess as to why you think God made Moses write out on stone tablets the Ten Commandments?
- List a few writings that are being disseminated in your workplace. How could they be better? Do they enable or hinder you as a leader or employee? What would you do differently?

Land

- What issues do you face in written communication as a leader?
- What steps do you need to take to overcome these issues?

Do

- Take 15 minutes each day this week to write with excellence.

Cultural Intelligence

"Strength lies in our differences, not our similarities."

—STEPHEN COVEY

"When pride comes, then comes disgrace,
but with the humble is wisdom."

—PROVERBS 11:2

It's more than classroom education—it's real-world education

Classroom education and business acumen will contribute to your leadership development, but in today's world you need more than just these two elements. Leadership today has many more high-touch experiences with stakeholders and leaders at every level than in preceding decades. Add to this that leaders need to be able to maneuver ever-changing cultural settings. You cannot miss the fact that as your world "gets smaller" business is becoming more globally founded; leaders must be able to understand, appreciate, and support these differences to lead effectively.

Cultural intelligence is the ability to negotiate cultural practices, leadership nuances, team distinctions, and communication diversity. These skills are learned while interacting with culture. These abilities are intricate to bridge, yet critical to understand and can strengthen or weaken alliances. Leaders who actively grow their cultural intelligence are in stronger positions to lead through changing circumstances. Here are three postures of the culturally intelligent leader.

Three Postures of a Leader

Posture One | Humility

Leaders who are overconfident are destined to fall. The question is usually how far and how hard. Hubris keeps a leader self-focused and prohibits them from listening carefully to cultural nuances, but humility works hard to be others-focused, taking the position of a learner. Cultural intelligence requires the humility to understand that although you hold some level of expertise in your role and position, you don't know all things about all cultures. It assumes that while a solution, system, sequence, or segmentation works well in one culture, the same implementation may not work well in another.

Posture Two | Curious

Humility gives way to a leader being curious. The best thing you can do in a cross-cultural situation is to ask a lot of questions and draw people out rather than to talk about ourselves, your methods, and your ideas. In your questions, you should seek to understand, not merely to be understood. You may even need to yield your cultural ignorance or inexperience to build a meaningful connection with others. The more time you spend with someone of another culture, the more you will become sensitive to other cultures and recognize how much you may not know. Such a leader is willing to invite questions and discussion, knowing they may create the best exchange. Being able to encourage others to share their viewpoints is an art in every culture. Keep in mind that, in some cultures, employees are not allowed to challenge a process, and others make decisions by consensus. You don't know what you don't know, so be inquisitive.

Posture Three | Sensitive

In conversations and dialogue with those from another culture, whether in a group setting or one on one, it is essential to be sensitive to matters that could be inflammatory. For example, criticism of government, while fine in American culture, may be taboo in another. Remember that each cultural group has a unique worldview, and the fact that it is different from ours does not mean that it is wrong, just that it is different. Even countries that speak the same language—Canada, the United Kingdom, and Kenya, for instance, do not necessarily share the same worldview.

Remember this when interacting with those from a different culture:

- Our worldview is different.
- Our collective experiences are different.
- Our leadership practices are often different.
- Our practice family is often different.
- Our view of authority is different.
- Our social strata are different.
- Our politics are different.

All this is enough to suggest that humility, inquisitiveness, and sensitivity are critical components in developing cultural intelligence.

Reflection & Mentorship

Begin

- Classroom education and business acumen will contribute to your leadership success, but in today's world, you need cultural intelligence more than any time in history.

Unpack

- How is cultural intelligence vital to the growth of your role in your business?
- How could growth in this ability contribute to greater dividends in your personal or company mission?

Inform

- What does Covey mean in his quote above? Try stating what he says another way.
- How is pride "disgraceful" as referenced in the proverb above?
- The three postures above are soft skills. Why is cultural intelligence more of a soft skill than a hard skill? Or is it something different?

Land

- What issues do you need to address in your cultural communication?
- What steps do you need to take to be more effective in communicating cross-culturally?

Do

- Meet someone of another culture, religion, or different life experience and learn about their life and leadership.

Relentless Focus

"The successful warrior is the average man, with laser-like focus."

—BRUCE LEE

"Let your eyes look directly forward,
and your gaze be straight before you."

—PROVERBS 4:25

Focus is why some leaders accomplish more than others

It is always intriguing what some people accomplish in their lifetime. Some people achieve a great deal more than others—significantly more. Everyone is given the same amount of time every day. And everyone has intermittent issues and thus have varied levels of busyness. But what factors distinguish those who consistently accomplish more than others? Do they have higher giftedness, greater intelligence, or are they more in tune with themselves—or is there another factor?

The answer is quite simple. These leaders are far more focused than the average leader. They have an intense clarity about the opportunities and time they are given. Thus they are able to deliberately accomplish more than others who may invest time frivolously. They following are a few factors that contribute to your leadership focus and increase levels of productivity.

Three Factors to Leadership Focus

Factor One | Clarity

Clarity is a discipline. It lets us know what you want to go after in our life and work. If you lead a family, team, or organization, you can stay very busy doing all kinds of irrelevant activities, and most people know what this is like and how it feels. Or you can identify those things that should be your responsibility, allowing you to help others meet their objectives. The reason many leaders struggle to attain clarity is that it requires some deep reflection, honesty, self realization, and feedback to hone in this discipline. It is far easier to be attracted to immediate and urgent concerns than it is to clarify what is essential for you and your team members to undertake. A disposition for personal clarity is of primary importance to the leader, and you will find that your people crave a clear-eyed leader in a time of uncertainty.

Factor Two | Less is more

A leadership mindset that is focused on fewer priorities, but priorities of maximum importance, will by nature address other minor interruptions. The "less is more" precept is always stirring around in the back of a leader's mind. With a bit of strategic thinking, they understand that focusing on doing first things first will clear the way to tackle bigger issues, keeping the team from running from one small issue to another. If two leaders of equal talent, enthusiasm, and experience work the same business market in the same manner, but one focuses 100% of his time on activities that lead to results, who do you think is going to win out? Getting things done is not the focus of a great leader; it's accomplishing the right objectives. Zig Ziglar said years ago, "Lack of direction, not lack of time, is the problem." There are far too many distractions day to day. Those I know who focus on these few essential things always achieve far more than others.

Factor Three | Evaluate

The best leaders continually evaluate their time and work priorities. This is done to keep the main objective as the top priority and prevent their time being absorbed by less important things. They evaluate their time commitments carefully to ensure that what they say yes to is consistent with their key objectives. They will say no often—but with good reason. They may use the word no frequently in order to increase time or effort in another area. Steve Jobs said, "Focusing is about saying no." Weekly, monthly, and annually a leader should take time to evaluate their objectives, aligning with what is most important. You should be willing to stop doing those things that do not contribute to your goals.

If you practice these simple principles, you will be amazed at how much more productive you—and by extension your team, will become.

Reflection & Mentorship

Begin

- The focused leader is one who has an intense clarity, concentrates on less, and evaluates driving objectives; this frees the leader to accomplish more.

Unpack

- How often do you feel like you are simply running from one problem to the next?
- When this happens, how does it leave you feeling as a leader?

Inform

- Bruce Lee's quote is interesting as it comes from a man enormously accomplished in his field. Why does a warrior need focus?

- The proverb above commands us to let "your gaze be straight before you." What is your gaze focused on today?
- Of the three factors, which is hardest for you?

Land

- What issues do you need to address in your leadership focus?
- What steps do you need to take to be more focused today?

Do

- Try to use the word no five times this week and see if it impacts your leadership focus.

Continuous Improvement

"You don't learn to walk by following rules.
You learn by doing, and by falling over."

—RICHARD BRANSON

'Let the wise hear and increase in learning, and the one
who understands obtain guidance."

—PROVERBS 1:5

Our fast-paced world requires leaders who improve continuously

Leaders who lack a disposition for disciplined growth in today's business world will suffer the fate of professional suicide. Many jobs and job levels that were once considered to be permanent occupations in the business world are now changing faster due to technological innovation and globalization, which is driving organizations toward flatter and leaner models. Soft skills in the areas of cultural intelligence and emotional intelligence, unheard of not too long ago, are now considered critical leadership skills. The pace of networking and marketing in a web-driven social media environment are steadily shifting and expanding the marketplace as people worldwide get connected. And with this challenge comes change to how leadership is being accomplished—at lightning speed nonetheless. As John Kotter has said, "As the pace of change accelerates, there is naturally a greater need for effective leadership." And the way you address this is through improvement and growth.

Three Principles of Continuous Improvement

Principle One | Aim for there

Think about this: The education and skills that got you to your present position may not be enough to get you where you want to go. Every new level of leadership has its own set of challenges that require a new mindset and thus a new set of skills. As you face these challenges, you should welcome the opportunity to develop new paradigms that will accelerate your leadership. In the past, leaders would gain certification in a single field and then leverage that degree or certification for a lifetime. But in today's world, a person with a broad set of work experiences, many certifications, and numerous cultural experiences has the upper hand. You need to be able to prove to developing organizations that you have a drive for continuous learning and advancement. Companies and their leaders today know that the way business is being done is changing. They need employees with knowledge in new areas who can take on unique roles with new titles. Being committed to continuous learning has the power to take you to that new place others are looking to go.

Principle Two | Find mentors

Recruiting mentors—yes, more than one—is another way to drive for continuous improvement. No one person can mentor you in all areas. I have mentors I lean on for financial advice, spiritual advice, fitness advice, sales advice, personal advice, family advice, strategic advice, and parenting advice. You name it, and you can find a mentor. But you may have to do some convincing; many people will not think of themselves as a mentor. You need to look for people who do things you want to do, who know things you don't, who can accomplish great feats effortlessly. Engaging in multiple mentoring relationships with people who are a step or two ahead of you can help you learn things at a remarkable pace; no book you will ever read could induce such progress. Mentors can also help you understand how your work values need to change as you go from one level of responsibility to one higher. These are things you would not naturally know, as you have not had the relevant experience yet. So when initiating a relationship with a mentor, be very specific as to what you desire to gain from the time together, and be willing to read or participate in learning experiences that they recommend.

Principle Three | Read and ask questions

Ask your mentors, or those you respect, what books, articles, or journals they would recommend to you. Well-chosen books are far more critical than the number of books you read, although attempting to read at least one book per month is a good goal. It is said that Bill Gates reads about 50 books each year, and many great leaders have followed his lead. Also, strike up conversations with as many people as you can. And not just with senior-level leaders or those you want to mentor you, but with anyone who has done meaningful work in specific areas outside your expertise. Peter Drucker would spend up to an hour every morning talking to line managers in various industries to find out what was happening. He had a range of knowledge that was phenomenal, gleaned from conversations he had with people way down the line.

The bottom line is that leaders are learners—and they learn continuously and aggressively. The best leaders focus on growing holistically, honing their spiritual, emotional, relational, cultural, and work-related skills. The more you develop, the more you have to offer, and the more valuable you are to the organizations you serve.

Reflection & Mentorship

Begin

- In this fast-paced world, leaders must have a disposition for continuous improvement and growth.

Unpack

- Is continuous improvement critical to your role today? In what ways?
- How does a lack of continuous improvement and growth threaten your job and industry?
- Who is someone you know who is always improving? What type of things do they do to develop and grow?

Inform

- Richard Branson suggests you learn by "falling over." How have you "fallen over" lately, and what did you learn?
- The proverb above suggests you can obtain guidance. How is this done?
- Of the three principles, which one comes most naturally? Which one do you most need to develop?

Land

- What improvement challenges are you currently facing?
- What steps do you need to take to grow and improve?

Do

- Don't put off improvement; engage in one of the three principles above today.

Artful Delegation

"Surround yourself with the best people you can find,
delegate authority, and don't interfere as long as the
policy you've decided upon is being carried out."

—RONALD REAGAN

"Train up a child in the way he should go;
even when he is old he will not depart from it."

—PROVERBS 22:6

Stop procrastinating and start delegating

Delegation is a practice not quickly learned. Some interpret delegation as a show of personal weakness. Others fear tasks will not be done effectively or efficiently in the time it takes to just do them on their own. Whatever the reason, a lack of delegation keeps a leader from critical work, which is why delegation is both an art (that requires personal creativity) and discipline (that needs persistent action).

Keys to Delegation

One | Delegation is a necessity

The art of leadership includes the ability to focus on the most critical activities that will drive vision forward. But eventually, a growing leader will hit a natural limit–– time. Unless you can free up time, your leadership will get bogged down in activities that divert you from key priorities—especially in a season of growth and advancement. As a leader's responsibility grows, the only way to free up time for the critical issues is to delegate some key and important tasks to others who can do them.

A law that many ignore is that you cannot take on additional responsibility without relinquishing other responsibilities. Great leaders don't accomplish more because they do more, but because they do more of the right things. That is made possible only by delegating tasks, responsibilities, process, and control to others who are capable.

A good leadership principle is to ask yourself three questions periodically: What can I stop doing by delegating? What could I start doing by delegating? And what can I continue doing by delegating? Questions like this clarify what is essential for you in your leadership and allow you to focus, or refocus, on what is most important at this point in your leadership, management, or administration.

Two | Determine what to delegate

What you choose to delegate is essential. Some responsibilities should remain in your hands. This could include guarding the values and culture of the organization, delivering critical communications to staff, or maintaining knowledge of bottom-line metrics. Each leader needs to determine what is important to retain ownership and responsibility for, but these essential responsibilities usually include directional items.

For the rest, a general rule is that if someone else can do a task 80% as well as you, you should give it away so that you have time to focus on issues that will drive the enterprise forward. The mission, direction, and accomplishment of the organizational agenda is a leader's first responsibility, but can get lost in maintaining the status quo. You should be pushing yourself toward managing the future, not only the present, which means you must free up the necessary time to focus on this.

Three | Tactical considerations

First, ask your direct reports or an assistant whether there is anything you are doing that they could do for you. When you ask the staff if their talents are being fully utilized, they will almost always answer in the negative. Generally, a person's skills will develop faster than their responsibilities expand, and by posing the question, you'll get direct insight into what their new potential might be. It may be something you never would have considered on your own. This conversation will give you clues as to what you might delegate.

Second, load your calendar with the most important commitments first. Respect regular leadership work like important standing meetings, required communication, empowering others, and critical decisions that affect the organization's future.

Third, schedule space for reflection, thinking, and planning. Leaders need time to read, reflect, and focus on the future. This is one the most crucial missional activities of a leader and yet the most neglected. Most simply don't preserve the time—because they have not delegated.

After addressing these three priorities, anything that can be delegated should be. You aren't declaring these other tasks to be unimportant. But it is not necessary for you to do these tasks when someone else can.

All of us have a way of working to achieve results. Delegation requires that you give a task to someone else, clearly communicate the desired outcome, and provide the person with the freedom to accomplish the work in an agreed upon fashion. They may handle the process a little bit differently than you did, but if the needed outcome is achieved, then release it—and experience freedom. Being clear on the front end as to what you want will make the process easier for your delegate. But give it to someone who has the gifts and ability to accomplish the task. And be sure to give them credit for the work when it is done and express your appreciation for their contribution.

Remember that delegation is an art and a discipline. Artful in that it is different for each person, and a discipline in that it is going to require thinking and additional effort on your part. But in the end, it allows you as a leader to focus on the most important things, and it gives responsibility away to others who are also ready for a new challenge.

Reflection & Mentorship

Begin

- Delegation keeps a leader focused on critical work and is both an art (that requires personal creativity) and discipline (that needs persistent action).

Unpack

- How effectively do you delegate today on a scale of 1–10?
- What are your reasons for not delegating?
- There are people around you who are masterful at delegating. What types of things do they do that you can't—or merely have not tried before?

Inform

- Ronald Reagan was emphatic about delegation. When would he say would be the right time to interfere?

- The proverb above suggests that training will eventually pay off. Do you think you don't train, or delegate, because you think it won't pay off?
- Of the tactical considerations above, which one is the hardest for you in your current position?

Land

- What challenges do you presently face in successfully delegating?
- What steps do you need to take to overcome these challenges?

Do

- Delegate one task today. Don't put it off any longer.

Commitment Economy

"Unless commitment is made, there are only promises
and hopes... but no plans."

—PETER F. DRUCKER

"The plans of the diligent lead surely to abundance,
but everyone who is hasty comes only to poverty."

—PROVERBS 21:5

The economy of commitment

Every leader makes investments into their team and staff. Think of these as small deposits into an investment account. Sometimes you will make deposits and other times you will make withdrawals. Rather than exchanging money, your economy of exchange is trust. Therefore, when you keep a commitment to your team, a deposit of trust is made. When you break a commitment, a withdrawal of trust is required. Keep in mind, people invest in leaders who invest in them through a display of commitment. And since this commodity is always being exchanged, whether you see it or not, it's critical that you keep making investments into this account. The way you do this is by following through on spoken promises, verbal arrangements, and written commitments, because your leadership is only as valuable as the commitments you keep.

Everyone, not just leaders, should fulfill their obligations. However, when a staff member doesn't meet a deadline or follow through on a promise, they can likely be marginalized so that a few only feel the impact. But there is a different standard and economy for a leader. Leaders set the pace, example, and standard for everyone, and staff take their cues from their leaders on what is acceptable and what is not. If you are careless about commitments, your behavior will create a wake through the organization, and staff will take notice. No one comes under more scrutiny than a leader who does not follow through on their commitments.

Furthermore, leaders often talk to teams about fulfilling the promises they make to their constituents. Promises have little meaning if a leader has a marred history of not keeping their word. And a deficit of trust is hard to reconcile as teams seldom recover from a trust bankruptcy. It may seem like a small thing for a leader to be careless with commitments, but habitual carelessness has many irreconcilable costs.

What gets in the way of keeping your commitments?

It is helpful to reflect and process this because most leaders intend to follow through on their commitments, and yet many struggle to do so. There are several reasons why leaders have difficulty here.

One | Overcommitment

First, many leaders are overcommitted. They agree to do far too many things. Usually this is because they don't want to disappoint team members, or they're trying to impress a supervisor, and so they agree to a task without considering the time involved. But remember, you must consider not only the time necessary to fulfill the obligation, but also the preparation you'll need to do before getting started. When a deadline approaches, you won't want to discover that you don't have time to fulfill your commitment. And overcommitment is a reason for many broken promises.

Two | Disorganization

Second, some leaders are disorganized. This is why assistants are so valuable to a leader with remarkable gifts. They can organize the chaos surrounding the leader and manage the schedules of the more disorganized leaders. However, over-reliance on an assistant is unhealthy. Too much turmoil and disorganization can result in costly withdrawals in the economy of leadership. Every leader needs, in some way, to build the skill of organization.

Because neither of these excuses are disingenuous, it is easy for the leader to rationalize the behavior and consider broken commitments no big deal. But cumulatively, they are causing a loss of leadership capital. So here are two tools to lean on for increasing your commitment economy—and they are simple.

Tools for Keeping Commitments

One | Put it on your calendar

An essential tool for a leader is keeping an up-to-date calendar. If you view a leader's calendar, you'll see what is truly important to them. This may seem over-simplified but anything that is important will be found there, because your calendar is your tool. If it's important, it should be on your calendar. By extension, all commitments should move from verbal to written by putting it on a calendar along with the preparation time that's necessary to deliver on the commitment.

Two | Make thoughtful commitments

Leaders need to keep in mind that impulsive promises can be an enemy to commitment, because without careful thought you run the risk of not being able to deliver. Your calendar is usually going to be full, so if you are adding something, you also will need to subtract something. You are better served to make a note regarding any commitment under consideration and ensure that you can deliver before making it public. If you cannot make it happen on your calendar, it might be an unwise commitment to make.

Are you part of an organization that keeps its word both to one another and to your customers? Do you as a leader deliver on you promises to the people you report to and lead? Remember what's at stake: the economy of your leadership.

Reflection & Mentorship

Begin

- Leaders make commitments, and they're costly in the economy of leadership.

Unpack

- What are common reasons for the failure to keep commitments in your organization?
- What do these excuses communicate about the current challenges your company or team is facing?

Inform

- Peter Drucker says that commitment is equivalent to a plan. How does this reshape a corporate view of commitment?
- The proverb above says that planning leads to abundance and haste leads to poverty. How is this economy true in your leadership? How is this true in your workplace?

Land

- What commitment do you need to keep?
- What steps do you need to take to overcome the challenges this commitment presents?

Do

- Follow through and keep your word.

Leading Change

"Change your opinions, keep to your principles;
change your leaves, keep intact your roots."

—VICTOR HUGO

"Whoever isolates himself seeks his own desire;
he breaks out against all sound judgment."

—PROVERBS 18:1

Leading change is the test of your leadership

The ability to drive needed changes in a team or organization is a skill that all leaders must nurture. Understanding the strategic need for change is very different from the art of leading change. Many leaders are adept at the former but stumble at the latter. It's not unusual for teams to become cynical regarding change because it's often handled poorly. Change is a necessary part of leadership, so what are the principles for leading a healthy change process?

Principles for Leading Change

One | Understand with clarity everything that will change

Before entering a change process, a leader must understand precisely what needs to change, why it needs to change, and what things will look like on the other side of the change. It's tempting to enter change processes prematurely, knowing that change is needed without knowing what changes need to happen. The method of leading change is complicated, so don't complicate it further by operating without a clear vision of what will change and what will be unchanged.

Two | Prepare people emotionally for the change

Most people are naturally resistant to change. Thus, it is critical to prepare your team for the change and secondary changes that will follow. They need to understand why change is necessary, and you need to build a case for how that change will help the organization better accomplish its mission. In his book Leading Change, John Kotter suggests that if you can create a need that enables you to build a case for change, do so. Unless there is a cause compelling enough to change, people will naturally resist it for ease, comfort, and status quo.

Three | Always connect change to your mission and vision

Change for change's sake does not market well. You enter a change process so that you can meet the new challenges in a new environment to accomplish your mission and deliver on your brand promise. In many cases, a change is long overdue. The world has changed, but you have not. Your rationale for change must always be anchored in the mission and vision of the organization. After all, your mission is the reason for your existence. Always remind people of why your organization is changing: to ensure that together you accomplish your mission and vision in today's market.

This is one of the areas where a leader can defuse a crisis by explaining the implications of failure to change. What's at stake? The jobs of staff, the viability of the enterprise, and the future health of the company. In the end, you want to have convinced a majority of your team that this must happen and that the status quo is not an option.

Four | Recruit a team to guide the process

Before you enter the change process, ensure that you have the right people who will support the proposed changes. This is your support network that will guide the transition. There will inevitably be resistance to change along the way, and you need the right people with you to not only support the change but to be proponents for that change. That coalition needs to be strong enough to overcome the resistance that you will encounter in the process. Don't move forward without it.

Five | Provide ways for input

As you make a case over time for the coming changes, give your team the opportunity to weigh in and make additional suggestions. One of the best ways to do this is to dialogue over time with as many staff as you can. Explain when necessary, listen to issues they are encountering, invite dialogue on opportunities for adjustments, and listen to input, regardless of how it's delivered.

Remember that although you understand the need for change and what it will look like, many others will not. Even if you've spoken about it or written about it in a memo, this does not mean that constituents understand the change or the impact of the change. The more significant the change, the longer it takes for people to make the paradigm shift in their minds; many will not make the change until they see what life looks like on the other side of change. Be patient. Above all, listen and explain.

Six | In the process, overcommunicate

One cannot communicate enough in the process of change. Often, change is not just a different way of doing things but a significant paradigm shift. Communicate your case in as many different ways, settings, and communication modes as you can. Never assume that you have communicated enough. In your communications, find ways to keep the inevitable anxiety over change as low as possible. Your confidence in the process will give others confidence as well. Your communications, comments, and presence with staff will bring a needed level of stability to the process.

Seven | Persevere in resistance

You will encounter resistance to change. This may be active or passive resistance. You may have cynics on the staff. Some might even suggest that you are fixing something that isn't broken, giving you all kinds of grief and reasoning as to why this change is a bad idea. When such resistance comes, what your staff needs to hear you say is "We're resolved," and they also need to know you're not closing the debate out of stubbornness. You're acting out of a thoughtful resolve, fully aware that change is hard but is going to happen. You've committed to a direction you all need to go in together. And you are committed to completing the transition alongside your team, no one left behind. All too often, change stalls when resistance comes because leaders are intimidated and therefore question themselves. But if you have addressed the previous six points above, you don't need to harbor doubt. The resistance you're encountering is normal, and if you are clear on the what and the why, you will move forward, and hopefully others will too.

Reflection & Mentorship

Begin

- Leaders will face change and must lead it. The ability to drive needed changes in a team or organization is a skill that must be nurtured.

Unpack

- How often does your organization change?
- What are common reasons for these changes?
- Is it too much change or too little change? Why?

Inform

- Victor Hugo suggests some things should not change, like "principles." Can you think of examples of enduring principles?
- The proverb above suggests that "isolation" is not "sound." Why would this be?
- Which of the seven principles above caught your attention? Why?

Land

- What challenges do you face in an upcoming change? Is it a minor or major disruption of the status quo?
- What steps do you need to take to overcome these challenges personally? How can you help your team take the leap with you?

Do

- See change differently this week.